AMERICAN LANGUAGE REPRINTS

VOL. 35

RIDOUT'S VOCABULARY OF SHAWNEE

by

Thomas Ridout

Evolution Publishing
Merchantville, New Jersey

Reprinted from:

Matilda Edgar. 1890. *Ten Years of Upper Canada in Peace and War, 1805–1815; being the Ridout letters with Annotations*. Toronto: William Briggs.

This edition ©2006 by Evolution Publishing.
an imprint of Arx Publishing, LLC

Originally published in hardcover 2006.
Reprinted in paperback 2022.

Printed in the
United States of America

ISSN 1540-3475

ISBN 978-1-935228-26-4

CONTENTS

Preface to the 2006 edition

The Shawnee were an Algonquian tribe who originally inhabited the Ohio River Valley. Their precise home-
land is not known with certainty—by the time the
European colonial powers took more than a passing
notice of them in the mid-late 1600s, the tribe had already
been displaced and scattered by draining wars with the
Iroquois. But before another century had passed, a large
body of Shawnee eventually found their way back to the
Ohio country, where they were destined to have an
important impact in the shaping of the American frontier.

The most southerly of the Central Algonquian tribes—
their name comes from a root for "south"—the Shawnee
were related to their neighbors the Sauk, Fox and
Kickapoo, as well as the the Miami and Illinois. Through
association from time spent to the east in Pennsylvania,
they also enjoyed a close friendship with Eastern
Algonquian tribes like the Delawares.

Shawnee dialectology has not yet been systematically
analyzed, and compounding the issue is the fact that
extensive vocabularies of it only appear in the 1780s,
long after the tribe had already been subject to a good
deal of scattering and recombining. We know of five sub-
divisions of the Shawnee—*čalaka, kišpoko, mekoče,
pekowi* and *θawikila*—but it is not clear to what degree, if
any, these were separate linguistic varieties as well
(Callender 1978).

Thomas Ridout was born in Sherbourne, Dorsetshire,

England in 1754. Twenty years later he was sent to live with an elder brother in the Maryland colony, and during the turbulent years of the American Revolution he was employed in running trade vessels across the Atlantic. In January of 1788, he set out from Maryland on a journey out to the new wilderness settlement of Kentucky in order to collect from some of his debtors. He passed the remainder of the winter at Fort Pitt (now Pittsburgh), and set out on March 12th for the falls of the Ohio.

Traveling downriver on Good Friday near modern-day Portsmouth Ohio, Ridout and his party were captured by a war party comprised of Shawnee, Potawatomi, Ottawa and Cherokee. Ridout was then adopted by the Shawnee chief Kakinathucca and carried across Indiana towards the Wabash River and then up that river toward Fort Miami and Detroit where he was released four months later. During this time, he claimed to have "acquired a tolerable knowledge of their language, and began to understand them, as well as to make myself intelligible."

Kakinathucca's wife Metsigemewa apparently had a fondness for tea, and Ridout made particularly effective use of this trait in preserving a linguistic record of his captivity.

> "With the tea paper I made a book, stitched it with the bark of a tree, and with yellow ink of hickory ashes, mixed with a little water, and a pen made with a turkey quill, I wrote down the names of visible objects. The negro, in his moments of good humour, used to explain to me that which was difficult to be understood. In this manner I wrote two little books, which I carried in a

pocket I had torn from my breeches, and wore round
my waist tied by a piece of bark..."

The negro here referred to was a 25-year-old man
name Boatswain or Boosini, who was a fellow servant of
Kakinathucca but whom Ridout found "exceedingly inso-
lent." Nonetheless, Boosini seems to have had more than
a passing command of Shawnee—and without his help, it
is doubtful that Ridout could have been as effective in
committing the language to writing, given the compara-
tively short duration of his captivity.

Ridout's vocabulary, written in his tea paper book and
passed down to his descendants, was first printed as an
appendix to his letters in 1890. Of all the major Shawnee
vocabularies, his is one of the earliest; only Denny's of
1786 predates it (published as volume 14 in this series). A
brief header accompanying Ridout's list states: "Sundry
words of the Shawanese Language, the Orthography of
which is according to the English pronunciation," though
a few of the terms are noted specifically as being according to the French pronunciation. The native words were
originally arranged semantically; here the list has been
alphabetized and an English—Shawnee section has also
been added.

The relations between the Ohio Indians and the new
American nation had simmered to a boiling point by
1790. Settlers were streaming across the border and
claiming land over which the Shawnee still asserted
rights, leading to a series of frontier clashes between the
Americans and the Indians. Despite attempts on both

3

sides at avoiding open hostilities, war came. Major General Arthur St. Clair was sent on a punitive expedition into the Ohio country with a volatile mix of regular army and militia, amounting to 1400 men.

The St. Clair offensive was a disaster for the Americans. On November 4, 1791, the ragtag army was soundly defeated by 1000 Indians under the Miami war chief Little Turtle. According to Ridout, Kakinathucca had "a principal share" in the victory—but this Indian frontier success was short-lived. Ultimately, the American victory at the Battle of Fallen Timbers in 1794 ended the independent power of the Ohio Indians for good, clearing the way for American expansion into the Ohio country.

The tribe whose fortunes Ridout shared for those few months in 1788 was destined never again to enjoy the political prestige it held at the time of the Revolution. Internal divisions broke the Shawnee into separate political entities and scattered them once more. Even when their famed chief Tecumseh began to forge an alliance of tribes to resist white encroachment, many of the Shawnee of Ohio refused their support for his cause. Ultimately, these political divisions gave rise to the three separate groups known today: the Absentee Shawnee, the Cherokee Shawnee, and the Eastern Shawnee (Callender 1978).

Whatever the hostilities within the Shawnee nation and between it and the Americans, it was no doubt personal amity that impelled Kakinathucca in 1799 to visit

4

his old friend Ridout at the latter's house in York. The former captive introduced the Indian chief to his wife and children and expressed his own gratitude for the kind treatment he had received years before. It was probably the last they ever saw of each other. Kakinathucca died at Amherstberg around 1806, and Ridout died in 1829, having served in various political posts in Canada.

By the latter half of the 20th century there were only a few hundred native speakers of Shawnee left, but that time also happily coincided with a resurgence of interest in the language. Ronald Chrisley put together an eminently useful teaching manual in 1992, drawing from various early vocabularies including that of Ridout. Also, groups such as the Loyal Shawnee and Absentee Shawnee of Oklahoma have recently initiated language preservation programs. Thus, despite the dozens of relocations, removals and divisions of the Shawnee people over four centuries, their native language and culture remarkably continues to endure.

—Claudio R. Salvucci, series ed.

Bibliography and Recommended Reading

Callender, Charles. 1978. "Shawnee." in William Sturtevant, Bruce Trigger, eds., *Handbook of North American Indians vol. 15: Northeast*, pp. 622-635. Washington, D.C.:Smithsonian Institution.

Chrisley, Ronald L. 1992. *An Introduction to the Shawnee Language*. North Baltimore, OH:R. L. Chrisley.

Edgar, Matilda. 1890. *Ten Years of Upper Canada in Peace and War, 1805-1815; being the Ridout letters with Annotations*. Toronto:William Briggs.

Goddard, Ives. 1978. "Central Algonquian Languages." in William Sturtevant, Bruce Trigger, eds., *Handbook of North American Indians vol. 15: Northeast*, pp. 583-587. Washington, D.C.:Smithsonian Institution.

Goddard, Ives, ed. 1996. *Handbook of North American Indians vol. 17: Languages*. Washington, D.C.: Smithsonian Institution.

Hanna, Charles A. 1911. *The Wilderness Trail; or, the Ventures and Adventures of the Pennsylvania Traders on the Allegheny Path*. New York and London:G.P. Putnam's Sons.

Hunter, William A. 1978. "History of the Ohio Valley." in William Sturtevant, Bruce Trigger, eds., *Handbook of North American Indians vol. 15: Northeast*, pp. 588-593. Washington, D.C.:Smithsonian Institution.

Miller, Wick R. 1959. "An Outline of Shawnee Historical Phonology." *International Journal of American Linguistics* 25:16-21.

Parks, Douglas R. 1975. "Shawnee Noun Inflection." Pp. 135-161 in *Studies in Southeastern Indian Languages*. James M. Crawford, ed. Athens: University of Georgia Press.

Thomas, Cyrus. 1891. "The Story of a Mound; or, the Shawnees in Pre-Columbian Times." *American Anthropologist* 4(2):109-159, (3):237-273.

Voegelin, Charles F. 1935. "Shawnee Phonemes." *Language* 11(1):23-37.

Voegelin, Charles F. 1936. "Productive Paradigms in Shawnee." in Robert H. Lowie, ed., *Essays in Anthropology in Honor of Alfred Louis Kroeber*, pp. 391-403 Berkeley:University of California Press.

Voegelin, Charles F. 1938-1940. *Shawnee Stems and the Jacob P. Dunn Miami Dictionary.* Indiana Historical Society Prehistory Research Series 1:63-108, 135-167, 289-323, 345-406, 409-478.

Voegelin, Charles F. et al. 1954. "Shawnee Laws: Perceptual Statements for the Language and for the Content" Pp. 32-46 in *Language in Culture. Harry Hoijer*, ed. Chicago:University of Chicago Press. (Also published as Memoirs of the American Anthropological Association 79).

Excerpt from
Narrative of the Captivity among the Shawanese Indians, in 1788

We all remained silent, every one judging that his last moment of life approached. In a few minutes this savage returned and drove before him the man who had been sitting next to me on the left. Mr. Purviance then said to me, "I believe, my friend, that we draw near our end." These were my sentiments also. I waited the return of the Indian for myself as his next victim; words cannot express what my feelings then were, and when I saw him approach. He came and stood before me, and, after a moment's pause, beckoned me to rise and follow him, and turned round in to the woods which were behind us. I saw my friend no more. I understood some time after that he was not killed on the spot, but was taken into the interior of the country and there beat to death.

I followed the Indian step by step, expecting every moment that he would turn upon me and put me to death. After walking 300 or 400 yards, I perceived the smoke of a fire, and, presently, several Indians about it; my alarm was not diminished, but as we came nearer, a white man, about twenty-two years of age, who had been taken prisoner when a lad and had been adopted, and was now a chief among the Shawanese, stood up and said to me in English, "Don't be afraid, sir, you are in no danger, but are given to a good man, a chief of the Shawanese, who will not hurt you; but, after some time, will take you to

Detroit, where you may ransom yourself. Come and take your breakfast"…

Soon after the sun had risen, the Indian chief to whom I had been given made his appearance. He seemed about fifty years of age, was a tall, slender man, and of a very pleasing and animated countenance. He, smiling, took me by the hand, called me "Nacanah," or his friend, and seeing my attention fixed on a wound, over one of his eyes, he, pointing to it, said, "Ah! matowesa whiskey," meaning he had gotten drunk with wicked whiskey or spirits, and that the wound was the bad consequence of it.…

Upon our arrival, several chiefs, to the number of fifty or upwards, opened the council. My papers were read by an interpreter, a white man, who several years before had been taken prisoner. After much sober discussion, in which it was declared that I was an Englishman and not an American, they broke up, after allowing my master to take me to Detroit, and there to receive my ransom. Towards the evening there was a dance of young women before the council-house, to the beat of a drum and their voices. They made signs to me to join them, but my friend advised me not to go. I had by this time acquired a tolerable knowledge of their language, and began to understand them, as well as to make myself intelligible. My mistress, as I have before mentioned, loved her dish of tea. With the tea paper I made a book,* stitched it with the bark of a tree, and with yellow ink of hickory ashes,

---

* This book still remains in good preservation, to testify to Mr. Ridout's ingenuity. It is now in the possession of Mrs. Edgar, his granddaughter.

mixed with a little water, and a pen made with a turkey quill, I wrote down the names of visible objects. The negro, in his moments of good humour, used to explain to me that which was difficult to be understood. In this manner I wrote two little books, which I carried in a pocket I had torn from my breeches, and wore round my waist tied by a piece of bark; generally elm bark was used on such occasions, as it may be divided into numberless small strips, which are very strong....

We then rode along on the other side and passed a fine plantation well stocked with cattle, belonging to a Shawanese chief, called Blue Jacket. He commanded the party, who afterwards vanquished the American general, St. Clair.* We soon came to the house of the Great Snake, who received me with kindness, and assured me of his protection. He was an elderly man, robust and rather corpulent. His wife, a pretty, well-looking woman, nearly his age, walked very stately with a handsome staff with a head to it. He ordered a bear's skin and blanket for me, alongside his own bed, and till my departure, three days after, he treated me with the greatest kindness. During this time I was informed that another council would be held upon me, whether I should be permitted to be taken to Detroit and ransomed. The day accordingly came in which the council was to be held. The Indians having assembled, I was also conducted thither. The council was under the authority of a Captain John, a Shawanese chief, before whom my case was to be decided. One Simon Girty, an Indian interpreter, now living on the Detroit

---

* November, 1791.

river, was present. I perceived that my master and friend was much dejected, and did not speak to me. Several women endeavoured to cheer me by saying I should not be hurt. The council was at length opened, and the Indian who had burned Mitchell contended for me. He insisted that I was a spy and that I knew the whole country. Much was said, and my papers and letters were again brought forward, read, and explained. At lengths, after a cool and deliberate hearing, the chief pronounced my discharge, and told my friend that he might set out with me as soon as he chose. His eyes sparkled with joy when relating the result of the deliberation of the council. He would have deferred our departure till the morrow, for the Indian traders who lived on the other side of a river which also formed a junction here with the other two, had long expected me, but dared not intercede for me whilst my life was at issue. After urging with all my power to set off immediately, my friend got a canoe and took me over to the traders' village, called Fort Miami; and both the English and French gentlemen were waiting, with open arms to receive me, as they had been acquainted with the chief's decision in my favour.

—Thomas Ridout, 1788.

SHAWNEE—ENGLISH

A-a, *yes.*
Ala-aqua, *the stars.*
Alequenenthequa, *will they kill me.*
Alla-luey, *'tis very unfortunate.*
Allicaw Paw keeta, *throw it away.*
Alloley, *a bullet.*
Allotheka, *the sunshine.*
Ameaqua, *a beaver.*
Assiskee, *earth.*
Atchsemo, *to speak.*
Awkitawkeloukee, *are you sick.*
Awkitsee, *a turkey-cock.*
Awquaw-tegtee, *heat of the sun.*
Awquiloukee, *sick.*
Awsit-thekee, *crosses worn on the neck.*

Catawaypetheaway, *the head.*
Catawelegnee, *a Negro.*
Cawwimeysa, *thorny locust tree.*
Cawwinakee, *thorny locust bean.*
Chagathwey, *nine.*
Chawaka tepea-away, *eight hundred.*
Chawa-ka, *ninety.*
Cheeakee, *we or all.*
Chepcock, *Port St. Vincent on the Wabash.*
Chiakee, *we, or all are sick.*
Cockelamoutha, *a hen.*
Coonee, *snow.*

Coquaw, *a pot, or kettle.*
Coqueo, *I don't care.*
Coupelecou, *iron.*
Cowasquee, *wheat.*
Cuttey-waw, *black.*

Eameetha, *a sister.*
Eleckhaalee, *go away.*
Elena lui, *an arrow.*
Elenaquey, *a bow.*
Eleney, *a man.*
Enee, *yes.*
Enou Kee-mehee, *a little while ago.*
Enoukee, *today.*
Eyawpee, *a buck.*

Geemewawnee, *rain.*
Goulaka, *a basin, or dish.*

Hamquaw, *a spoon.*
Hattawa, *punk.*
Hoosstou, *to make.*

Jackqueleymaw, *I love you.*

Ka-anah, *friend.*
Kakawkee, *a raven.*
Kalipatchehee, *never mind it.*

Kataqueleymawtee, *do you love me.*

Kawcoa, *a razor.*

Kawqua, *a porcupine.*

Kealaw, *you.*

Keekaatsee, *the leg.*

Keelanee, *tongue.*

Keepetsee, *teeth.*

Keetawnenah, *mouth.*

Kegsetee, *hot, as water.*

Keisekelaqua, *Venus, the planet.*

Keisewaquata, *the sycamore.*

Keletsapethou, *a ring.*

Keletsee, *fingers.*

Kenekee, *arm.*

Kesekee-kasothwaw, *the sun.*

Kesothwa, *a moon, or month.*

Kessekee, *day.*

Ketchena, *thumb.*

Kethenequa, *soap.*

Ketheney, *to wash.*

Kethetena, *the foot.*

Kethwee, *how many.*

Keweeakouah, *are you angry.*

Kicotto, *a year.*

Kikawka-mackee, *Detroit.*

Kikenecaw, *a prisoner.*

Kincapethou, *a bracelet.*

Kipscawquee, *to choke.*

Kitellee, *to tell.*

Kitsecommey, *the sea, or a lake.*

Kitsetheynaweisa, *the bark.*

Kittatee, *an otter.*

Kusko, *hog.*

Kuskokee, *hogs.*

Lami, *very.*

Lamouesa, *very good.*

Lamyolethey, *very pretty.*

Lamyouesa, *very good.*

Laquyawaw, *where is he gone?*

Leakaw, *a goose.*

Leewawtey, *smoke of a fire.*

Lenawpey, *a Delaware.*

Leykuckee, *last night.*

Leynowakee, *an Indian.*

Loucanah, *flour.*

Maaquaw, *a bear.*

Macota, *the women's petticoat.*

Macouteley-tha, *a fawn or colt.*

Makalitou, *a frog.*

Makeytha, *a sheep.*

Manitou-wawquemeysee, *buckeye tree.*

Masisskee, *tea.*

Matow-e-hahee, *nothing.*

Matowessa, *bad.*

Mattapelou, *sit down*.

Maw, *take*.

Mawweeachee, *that way*.

Meakeybue-thetha, *an old woman*.

Mealawqua, *ash*.

Mecothey, *an awl*.

Mecottey, *gunpowder*.

Meeasathucckee, *Irish potatoes*.

Meeawee, *a path, or road*.

Meeaw-neequaw, *a young woman*.

Meeaw-nelenee, *a young man*.

Melassey, *sugar*.

Meleynawpee, *milk*.

Melocaummee, *spring*.

Memeaquee, *to run*.

Menealapee, *to dance*.

Mesisskee, *a leaf or herb*.

Metaghtheney ketenchawgaththwea, *nineteen*.

Metaghtheney keteneallauwey, *fifteen*.

Metaghtheney keteneawey, *fourteen*.

Metaghtheney ketenecoutothwey, *sixteen*.

Metaghtheney ketenesoythwey, *seventeen*.

Metaghtheney keteneycoutey, *eleven*.

Metaghtheney keteneyswee, *twelve*.

Metaghtheney ketensoyuricothwey, *eighteen*.

Metaghtheney ketenthwea, *thirteen*.

Metaghthwey, *ten*.

Metagththeney tepea-away, *one thousand*.

Methalui, *lead.*

Metsemee, *moon.*

Metsemee, *no moon.*

Metsy, *many.*

Metticoseeah, *a white man, or Englishman.*

Mine-athey, *an island.*

Moketha, *moccasins.*

Mokita, *leggings.*

Monathee, *a knife.*

Monspethey, *tall.*

Mosco, *a Creek Indian.*

Mutchamanitoo, *the devil.*

Mutta teibois, *'tis not true.* (Fr. pro.)

Mutta, *no.*

Muttalaqua, *not any—no more.*

Mutta-nawacouta, *I don't know it.*

Nacommo, *to sing.*

Nameatha, *a fish.*

Nawacouta, *I know it.*

Nawpeya, *a cock.*

Neaallanwawpetockkee, *fifty.*

Neabeakee, *summer.*

Neakea, *a mother.*

Nealanawey, *five.*

Nealaw, *I.*

Neallany tepea-away, *five hundred.*

Neapouthou, *to burn.*

Neaqueytha, *my son.*

Neasinee tepea-away, *two hundred.*

Neasit-chee, *a husband.*

Neaswawpeatatache, *twenty.*

Neawai, *I thank you.*

Neawaw, *a wife.*

Neawee tepea-away, *four hundred.*

Neawee, *four.*

Necotothwey, *six.*

Necounakikee, *two days hence.*

Necoutothwey, *twenty.*

Necoutoyththeni tepea-away, *six hundred.*

Neekatyawsee, *sixty.*

Neepee, *water.*

Neesyawsee, *seventy.*

Neetsawsee, *nose.*

Neheeway, *how do you call that?*

Nekaanah, *my friend.*

Neleytha, *the hair.*

Neloutsy, *for nothing.*

Nelowto, *a captain.*

Nemenee, *to drink.*

Nenesacou, *two days ago.*

Nenimkee, *thunder.*

Nenimkee-wanwee, *loud thunder.*

Nensweleymaw, *I love you.*

Nepaalo, *lie down.*

Nepepemee, *salt.*

Nepey-waw, *sleep*.

Nepouah, *dead*.

Neseeno, *twice*.

Nesothwey, *seven*.

Nessoyththeni tepea-away, *seven hundred*.

Neteibois, *I tell true*. (Fr. pro.)

Netessatahai, *I think so*.

Neuatchsemo, *to speak false*.

Newawpetockkee, *forty*.

Nicoutee, *one*.

Nisswee, *two*.

Nonolaweisky, *the north star*.

Notha, *a father*.

Notob-oley, *war*.

Nottowei, *a Mohawk*.

Nottoweitha, *a Wyandot*.

Nounouconwey, *a swamp*.

Okemah, *a king*.

Olethey quiawa, *pretty woman*.

Olethey, *pretty*.

Oucahounie, *a fort*.

Oucahounie, *Fort Mattawa*.

Ou-ecawteke, *a book, letter, or map*.

Ouesa, *good*.

Ouey, *done, or dressed*.

Oulacon, *yesterday*.

Oulageysee, *a canoe*.

Oulamon, *vermillion*.

Ouskipemee, *sweet corn*.

Outatsica, *stem of the pipe*.

Outhaw-wee, *yellow*.

Outhaw-wee monie, *gold, or yellow money*.

Pakitchee, *gone away*.

Papaqueymee, *cranberries*.

Papiache, *I will*.

Pasquemei, *a mosquito*.

Passitotha, *an old man*.

Pawpiachee, *I will*.

Pawquanemeysee, *sassafras*.

Pea-atcho, *give me*.

Pealeywaw, *a turkey-hen*.

Pealouee, *a great way off*.

Peaquelineykee, *the Pleiads*.

Peccouai, *town*.

Peealo, *come here*.

Peeawaw, *they are coming*.

Peletsewah, *hand*.

Peliko, *once*.

Peloutsy, *by and by*.

Peloutsyhea, *presently*.

Pemee, *bear's oil*.

Pemoutee, *to walk*.

Pemqua Teaquah, *a rifle*.

Peneeakee, *wild potatoes*.

23

Pepapaunwey, *lightning.*

Pepokee, *winter.*

Pesalo, *take care.*

Pesseywaw, *a wild cat.*

Petacouah, *a hat, or cap.*

Pete keneth pia, *when will he come back?*

Peteyway, *smoke of a pipe or tobacco.*

Petheawai, *a breast-plate, or gorget.*

Petsoie, *wampum.* (Fr. pronoun)

Peyteneekah, *a shirt, or jacket.*

Pitssawkah, *a rope, or halter.*

Poconuey, *a wave.*

Poosica, *a cat.*

Poppea-awai, *a saddle.*

Popsquawsewaymeysee, *beech.*

Poutala, *a skin for carrying oil.*

Pouthquatee, *cloudy.*

Poweatha, *a pigeon.*

Pyawaw, *here.*

Quacah, *a pipe.*

Quala-aqua, *Ursa Major.*

Quass-quetuckkee, *a cataract, or falls.*

Quaw-ma, *ice.*

Quaw-melaw-nee, *hail.*

Quawnikee, *a chain.*

Queakee, *woman.*

Queekaca, *neck.*

Queg-awai, *a blanket*.

Quiawaw, *a woman*.

Sacouka, *a flint*.

Satewei, *a rattlesnake*.

Saw-wee, *big*.

Scootee, *fire*.

Scothakeweitamee, *will you be my wife*.

Scoute-cagah, *steel for striking fire*.

Scoutelawmee, *a tortoise*.

Scoutseathawpou, *coffee*.

Sea-a-way, *a horse*.

Seapessee, *a panther*.

Seaseepa, *a duck*.

Secacoonee, *wind*.

Seckthee, *a deer*.

Seeaway kee, *horses*.

Seeaway, *a horse*.

Sequaw, *cedar*.

Sequawna, *a stone*.

Setaquotha, *leather*.

Shemanthee, *a Virginian*.

Showanyaw, *a Shawanese*.

Simmenachkee, *an apple*.

Skeaquee, *a pond of water*.

Skelouatheatha, *a boy*.

Skesaquey, *the eye*.

Skippeimeysee, *hickory*.

Sonlageysee, *a ship.*

Spaniee, *a Spaniard.*

Speleawee-thepee, *Ohio river.*

Spemmekee, *on the top.*

Spemme-kee, *on the top.*

Squatawmeysee, *shell-bark hickory.*

Squathapeah, *a belt.*

Squawlawey, *I am hungry.*

Squawthee, *little.*

Squaw-wee, *red.*

Squee, *blood.*

Squeytheatha, *a girl.*

Squimenuckee, *haws.*

Sweagetissetha, *what is your name?*

Taa-neweikata, *where are you going?*

Tat-chimokee, *a council.*

Ta-winikee, *a town.*

Tawmey, *Indian corn.*

Tawnewee, *let me see.*

Tawneweicoomah, *where do you come from?*

Tawney, *where is it.*

Tawneytha, *my daughter.*

Tawqueloukee, *I am sick.*

Teaquah, *a gun.*

Teaquawko, *autumn.*

Teaque matta nemeta, *don't give it.*

Teaquea-atchsimo, *don't tell.*

Teaquee, *a tree.*

Teaque-weitemaha, *don't tell him of it.*

Teatepawtaquey, *the vine.*

Teekhauhka, *tomahawk.*

Teikou, *wood for fire.*

Teneetsup, *it is true.*

Tepea-away, *one hundred.*

Tepeykee kasothwaw, *the moon.*

Tepeykee, *night.*

Tepthicah, *a cup, or teapot.*

Teypatuca, *Orion's Belt.*

Thakoa, *a shirt broach.*

Thawkee, *new moon, or come out.*

Thawthicatsica, *a frying-pan.*

Theaquee, *to kill.*

Theckthey, *deer sinews.*

Thecounakikee, *three days hence.*

Theemeytha, *a brother.*

Theepaatee, *a raccoon.*

Thenee tepea-away, *three hundred.*

Thenomeysee, *the sugar tree.*

Thepee, *a river.*

Thequa, *a comb.*

They-amah, *tobacco.*

Theywe, *three.*

Thotho, *a cow.*

Thowthyaw, *a buffalo.*

Thya, *a skin.*

Thyawpeytockkee, *thirty.*
Thyawsee, *eighty.*
Thyawsicthewy, *eight.*
Tike commee, *a spring of water.*
Toete, *a Frenchman.*
Tow-waaka, *the ear.*

Wanatho, *he is drunk.*
Wanesucca, *a fool.*
Waupamoua, *a looking-glass.*
Waw-connokee-wapea, *white.*
Wawcouchee, *a fox.*
Wawkitomica-thepee, *Muskingum river.*
Wawpackee, *tomorrow.*
Wawpaquemeysee, *white oak.*
Wawpatheea, *a swan.*
Wawpauwey, *daylight.*
Waw-wee, *an egg.*
Weapee, *cold.*
Weeawthey, *venison, or meat.*
Weela, *he or him.*
Weelenoix, *fat.*   (Fr. pron.)
Weethuckapee, *rum.*
Weewilsquee, *the capillaire plant.*
Wei-coupee, *bark to tie with.*
Weilawnahai, *ginseng.*
Weisamanitoo, *God.*
Wessee-aw, *husband.*

Wessitic, *a mountain.*

Wetchewai Scup-qua, *'tis so.*

Wetchewai, *let it be so.*

Wetheneto, *eat some.*

Wewawlee, *my wife.*

Weweyla, *a powder horn.*

Weykeewaw, *a house.*

Weynussee, *a turkey-buzzard, a vulture.*

Wiapawkekee, *silver dollars, or white money.*

Wiapawke-quaw, *tin.*

Winussey, *a scalp.*

Wiskeloutha, *a bird.*

Withaw-waw-caquaw, *brass.*

Wya-pe-tee-et, *an elk.*

Wyeewaw, *a wolf.*

Wyschchee, *a dog.*

Wythaw-quawkey-quaw, *a bottle.*

Wythaw-wicommikee, *Fort Pitt.*

Yawmah, *he, or it.*

Yawmawqueloukee, *he is sick.*

ENGLISH—SHAWNEE

Ago, a little while ago, *enou kee-mehee.*

All, *cheeakee.*

Angry, are you angry?, *keweeakouah.*

Apple, an, *simmenachkee.*

Arm, *kenekee.*

Arrow, an, *elenlui.*

Ash, *mealawqua.*

Autumn, *teaquawko.*

Awl, an, *mecothey.*

Bad, *matowessa.*

Bark, the, *kitsetheynaweisa.*   **To tie with bark,** *wei-coupee.*

Basin, a, *goulaka.*

Bear, a, *maaquaw.*

Bear's oil, *pemee.*

Beaver, a, *ameaqua.*

Beech, *popsquawsewaymeysee.*

Belt, a, *squathapeah.*

Big, *saw-wee.*

Bird, a, *wiskeloutha.*

Black, *cuttey-waw.*

Blanket, a, *queg-awai.*

Blood, *squee.*

Book, a, *ou-ecawteke.*

Bottle, a, *wythaw-quawkey-quaw.*

Bow, a, *elenaquey.*

Boy, a, *skelouatheatha.*

33

Bracelet, a, *kincapethou.*

Brass, *withaw-waw-caquaw.*

Breast-plate, a, *petheawai.*

Broach, a shirt broach, *thakoa.*

Brother, a, *theemeytha.*

Buck, a, *eyawpee.*

Buckeye tree, *manitou-wawquemeysee.*

Buffalo, a, *thowthyaw.*

Bullet, a*, alloley.*

Burn, to, *neapouthou.*

By and by, *peloutsy.*

Call, how do you call that?, *neheeway.*

Canoe, a, *oulageysee.*

Cap, *petacouah.*

Capillaire plant, the, *weewilsquee.*

Captain, a, *nelowto.*

Care, take care, *pesalo.* **I don't care,** *coqueo.*

Cat, a, *poosica.* **A wild cat,** *pesseywaw.*

Cataract, a, *quass-quetuckkee.*

Cedar, *sequaw.*

Chain, a, *quawnikee.*

Choke, to, *kipscawquee.*

Cloudy, *pouthquatee.*

Cock, a, *nawpeya.*

Coffee, *scoutseathawpou.*

Cold, *weapee.*

Colt, a, *macouteley-tha.*

Comb, a, *thequa.*

Come here, *peealo.* **Come out,** *thawkee.* **They are com-ing,** *peeawaw.* **When will he come back?,** *pete keneth pia.* **Come, where do you come from,** *tawneweicoom-ah.*

Corn, Indian corn, *tawmey.* **Sweet corn,** *ouskipemee.*

Council, a, *tat-chimokee.*

Cow, a, *thotho.*

Cranberries, *papaqueymee.*

Creek Indian, a, *mosco.*

Crosses worn on the neck, *awsit-thekee.*

Cup, a, *tepthicah.*

Dance, to, *menealapee.*

Daughter, my, *tawneytha.*

Day, *kessekee.* **Two days ago,** *nenesacou.* **Two days hence,** *necounakikee.* **Three days hence,** *thecounaki-kee.*

Daylight, *wawpauwey.*

Dead, *nepouah.*

Deer, a, *seckthee.* **Deer sinews,** *theckthey.*

Delaware, a, *lenawpey.*

Detroit, *kikawka-mackee.*

Devil, the, *mutchamanitoo.*

Dish, *goulaka.*

Dog, a, *wyschchee.*

Done, *ouey.*

Dollars, silver dollars or white money, *wiapawkekee.*

35

Dressed, *ouey.*
Drink, to, *nemenee.*
Drunk, he is drunk, *wanatho.*
Duck, a, *seaseepa.*

Ear, the, *tow-waaka.*
Earth, *assiskee.*
Eat some, *wetheneto.*
Egg, an, *waw-wee.*
Eight, *thyawsicthewy.*
Eight hundred, *chawaktepea-away.*
Eighteen, *metaghtheney ketensoyuricothwey.*
Eighty, *thyawsee.*
Eleven, *metaghtheney keteneycoutey.*
Elk, an, *wya-pe-tee-et.*
Englishman, an, *metticoseeah.*
Eye, the, *skesaquey.*

Falls, *quass-quetuckkee.*
Fat, *weelenoix* (Fr. Pron.).
Father, a, *notha.*
Fawn, *macouteley-tha.*
Fifteen, *metaghtheney keteneallauwey.*
Fifty, *neaallanwawpetockkee.*
Fingers, *keletsee.*
Fire, *scootee.*
Fish, a, *nameatha.*
Five, *nealanawey.*

Five hundred, *neallany tepea-away.*

Flint, a, *sacouka.*

Flour, *loucanah.*

Fool, a, *wanesucca.*

Foot, the, *kethetena.*

Fort, a, *oucahounie.* **Fort Mattawa,** *oucahounie.* **Fort Pitt,** *wythaw-wicommikee.*

Forty, *newawpetockkee.*

Four, *neawee.*

Four hundred, *neawee tepea-away.*

Fourteen, *metaghtheney keteneawey.*

Fox, a, *wawcouchee.*

Frenchman, a, *toete.*

Friend, *ka-anah.* **My friend,** *nekaanah.*

Frog, a, *makalitou.*

Frying-pan, a, *thawthicatsica.*

Ginseng, *weilawnahai.*

Girl, a, *squeytheatha.*

Give me, *pea-atcho.* **Don't give it,** *teaque mattnemeta.*

Go away, *eleckhaalee.* **Gone away,** *pakitchee.* **Where are you going?,** *taa-neweikata.* **Where is he gone?,** *laquyawaw.*

God, *weisamanitoo.*

Gold, or yellow money, *outhaw-wee monie.*

Good, *ouesa.* **Very good,** *lamyouesa* or *lamouesa.*

Goose, a, *leakaw.*

Gorget, *petheawai.*

Gun, a, *teaquah.*
Gunpowder, *mecottey.*

Hail, *quaw-melaw-nee.*
Hair, the, *neleytha.*
Halter, *pitssawkah.*
Hand, *peletsewah.*
Hat, a, *petacouah.*
Haws, *squimenuckee.*
He, *weela, yawmah.*
Head, the, *catawaypetheaway.*
Heat of the sun, *awquaw-tegtee.*
Hen, a, *cockelamoutha.*
Herb, an, *mesisskee.*
Here, *pyawaw.*
Hickory, *skippeimeysee.* **Shell-bark hickory,** *squatawmeysee.*
Him, *weela.*
Hog, *kusko.* **Hogs,** *kuskokee.*
Horn, a powder horn, *weweyla.*
Horse, a, *sea-a-way, seeaway.* **Horses,** *seeaway kee.*
Hot, as water, *kegsetee.*
House, a, *weykeewaw.*
How many, *kethwee.*
Hungry, I am hungry, *squawlawey.*
Husband, *wessee-aw.* **A husband,** *neasit-chee.*

I, *nealaw.*

Ice, *quaw-ma.*
Indian, an, *leynowakee.*
Iron, *coupelecou.*
Island, an, *mine-athey.*
It, *yawmah.*

Jacket, *peyteneekah.*

Kettle, *coquaw.*
Kill, to, *theaquee.* **Will they kill me?,** *alequenenthequa.*
King, a, *okemah.*
Knife, a, *monathee.*
Know, I know it, *nawacouta.* **I don't know it,** *mutta-nawacouta.*

Lake, a, *kitsecommey.*
Lead, *methalui.*
Leaf, a, *mesisskee.*
Leather, *setaquotha.*
Leg, the, *keekaatsee.*
Leggings, *mokita.*
Letter, *ou-ecawteke.*
Lie down, *nepaalo.*
Lightning, *pepapaunwey.*
Little, *squawthee.*
Locust, thorny locust tree, *cawwimeysa.* **Thorny locust bean,** *cawwinakee.*
Looking-glass, a, *waupamoua.*

Loud thunder, *nenimkee-wanwee.*

Love, I love you, *nensweleymaw,* *jackqueleymaw.* **Do you love me?,** *kataqueleymawtee.*

Make, to, *hoosstou.*

Man, a, *eleney.* **A young man,** *meeaw-nelenee.* **An old man,** *passitotha.*

Many, *metsy.* **Many, how many,** *kethwee.*

Map, *ou-ecawteke.*

Meat, *weeawthey.*

Milk, *meleynawpee.*

Mind, never mind it, *kalipatchehee.*

Moccasins, *moketha.*

Mohawk, a, *nottowei.*

Money, gold or yellow money, *outhaw-wee monie.* **Silver dollars or white money,** *wiapawkekee.*

Month, *kesothwa.*

Moon, *metsemee.* **The moon,** *tepeykee kasothwaw.* **A moon,** *kesothwa.* **No moon,** *metsemee.* **New moon, or come out,** *thawkee.*

More no more, *muttalaqua.*

Mosquito, a, *pasquemei.*

Mother, a, *neakea.*

Mountain, a, *wessitic.*

Mouth, *keetawnenah.*

Muskingum river, *wawkitomica-thepee.*

Name, what is your name?, *sweagetissetha.*

40

Neck, *queekaca.*
Negro, a, *catawelegnee.*
Night, *tepeykee.* **Last night,** *leykuckee.*
Nine, *chagathwey.*
Nineteen, *metaghtheney ketenchawgaththwea.*
Ninety, *chawa-ka.*
No, *mutta.*
North star, the, *nonolaweisky.*
Nose, *neetsawsee.*
Not any — no more, *muttalaqua.*
Nothing, *matow-e-hahee.* **For nothing,** *neloutsy.*

Oak, white, *wawpaquemeysee.*
Ohio river, *speleawee-thepee.*
Oil, bear's oil, *pemee.*
Old man, an, *passitotha.*
Old woman, an, *meakeybue-thetha.*
Once, *peliko.*
One, *nicoutee.*
One hundred, *tepea-away.*
One thousand, *metagththeney tepea-away.*
Orion's Belt, *teypatuca.*
Otter, an, *kittatee.*

Panther, a, *seapessee.*
Path, a, *meeawee.*
Petticoat, the women's petticoat, *macota.*
Pigeon, a, *poweatha.*

41

Pipe, a, *quacah.* **Stem of the pipe,** *outatsica.*

Planet, the planet Venus, *keisekelaqua.*

Pleiads, the, *peaquelineykee.*

Pond of water, a, *skeaquee.*

Porcupine, a, *kawqua.*

Port St. Vincent on the Wabash, *chepcock.*

Pot, a, *coquaw.*

Potatoes, wild, *peneeakee.* **Irish Potatoes,** *meeasathucc-kee.*

Powder horn, a, *weweyla.*

Presently, *peloutsyhea.*

Pretty, *olethey.* **Very pretty,** *lamyolethey.* **Pretty woman,** *olethey quiawa.*

Prisoner, a, *kikenecaw.*

Punk, *hattawa.*

Raccoon, a, *theepaatee.*

Rain, *geemewawnee.*

Rattlesnake, a, *satewei.*

Raven, a, *kakawkee.*

Razor, a, *kawcoa.*

Red, *squaw-wee.*

Rifle, a, *pemquteaquah.*

Ring, a, *keletsapethou.*

River, a, *thepee.*

Road, *meeawee.*

Rope, a, *pitssawkah.*

Rum, *weethuckapee.*

Run, to, *memeaquee.*

Saddle, a, *poppea-awai.*
Salt, *nepepemee.*
Sassafras, *pawquanemeysee.*
Scalp, a, *winussey.*
Sea, the, *kitsecommey.*
See, let me see, *tawnewee.*
Seven, *nesothwey.*
Seven hundred, *nessoyththeni tepea-away.*
Seventeen, *metaghtheney ketenesoythwey.*
Seventy, *neesyawsee.*
Shawanese, a, *showanyaw.*
Sheep, a, *makeytha.*
Shell-bark hickory, *squatawmeysee.*
Ship, a, *sonlageysee.*
Shirt, a, *peyteneekah.* **Shirt broach, a,** *thakoa.*
Sick, *awquiloukee.* **I am sick,** *tawqueloukee.* **Are you sick,** *awkitawkeloukee.* **He is sick,** *yawmawqueloukee.* **We, or all are sick,** *chiakee.*
Silver dollars, or white money, *wiapawkekee.*
Sinews, deer, *theckthey.*
Sing, to, *nacommo.*
Sister, a, *eameetha.*
Sit down, *mattapelou.*
Six, *necotothwey.*
Six hundred, *necoutoyththeni tepea-away.*
Sixteen, *metaghtheney ketenecoutothwey.*

Sixty, *neekatyawsee.*

Skin, a, *thya.* **Skin for carrying oil, a,** *poutala.*

Sleep, *nepey-waw.*

Smoke of fire, a, *leewawtey.* **Smoke of pipe or tobacco,** a, *peteyway.*

Snow, *coonee.*

So, let it be so, *wetchewai.* **'Tis so,** *wetchewai scup-qua.*

Soap, *kethenequa.*

Son, my, *neaqueytha.*

Spaniard, a, *spaniee.*

Speak, to, *atchsemo.* **To speak false,** *neuatchsemo.*

Spoon, a, *hamquaw.*

Spring, *melocaummee.*

Spring of water, a, *tike commee.*

Stars, the, *ala-aqua.* **The North star,** *nonolaweisky.* **Orion's Belt,** *teypatuca.* **The Pleiads,** *peaquelineykee.* **Ursa major,** *quala-aqua.*

Steel for striking fire, *scoute-cagah.*

Stone, a, *sequawna.*

Sugar, *melassey.*

Sugar tree, the, *thenomeysee.*

Summer, *neabeakee.*

Sun, the, *kesekee-kasothwaw.* **Heat of the sun,** *awquaw-tegtee.*

Sunshine, the, *allotheka.*

Swamp, a, *nounouconwey.*

Swan, a, *wawpatheea.*

Sycamore, the, *keisewaquata.*

44

Take, *maw.*

Tall, *monspethey.*

Tea, *masisskee.*

Teapot, *tepthicah.*

Teeth, *keepetsee.*

Tell, to, *kitellee.* **Don't tell***, a, teaquea-atchsimo.* **Don't tell him of it,** *teaque-weitemaha.*

Ten, *metaghthwey.*

Thank, I thank you, *neawai.*

Think, I think so, *netessatahai.*

Thirteen, *metaghtheney ketenthwea.*

Thirty, *thyawpeytockkee.*

Thorny locust bean, *cawwinakee.*

Thorny locust tree, *cawwimeysa.*

Three, *theywe.*

Three hundred, *thenee tepea-away.*

Throw it away, *allicaw paw keeta.*

Thumb, *ketchena.*

Thunder, *nenimkee.* **Loud thunder,** *nenimkee-wanwee.*

Tie, to tie with bark, *wei-coupee.*

Tin, *wiapawke-quaw.*

'Tis so, *wetchewai scup-qua.*

Tobacco, *they-amah.*

Today, *enoukee.*

Tomahawk, *teekhauhka.*

Tomorrow, *wawpackee.*

Tongue, *keelanee.*

Top, on the top, *spemmekee, spemme-kee.*

45

Tortoise, a, *scoutelawmee.*

Town, *peccouai.* **A town,** *ta-winikee.*

Tree, a, *teaquee.*

True, I tell true, *neteibois* (Fr. Pro.). **It is true**, *a, teneet-sup.* **'Tis not true,** *muttteibois* (fr. Pro.).

Turkey-cock, a, *awkitsee.*

Turkey-hen, a, *pealeywaw.*

Twelve, *metaghtheney keteneyswee.*

Twenty, *neaswawpeatatache* or *necoutothwey.*

Twice, *neseeno.*

Two, *nisswee.*

Two hundred, *neasinee tepea-away.*

Unfortunate, 'tis very, *alla-luey.*

Ursa major, *quala-aqua.*

Venison, *weeawthey.*

Venus, the planet, *keisekelaqua.*

Vermillion, *oulamon.*

Very, *lami.*

Vine, the, *teatepawtaquey.*

Virginian, a, *shemanthee.*

Vulture, a, *weynussee.*

Walk, to, *pemoutee.*

Wampum, *petsoie* (Fr. Pronoun).

War, *notob-oley.*

Wash, to, *ketheney.*

Water, *neepee.*

Wave, a, *poconuey.*

Way, that way, *mawweeachee.* **A great way off,** *peal-ouee.*

We, *cheeakee.*

Wheat, *cowasquee.*

Where is it, *tawney.*

White, *waw-connokee-wapea.* **Silver dollars or white money,** *wiapawkekee.* **White oak,** *wawpaquemeysee.*

Wife, a, *neawaw.* **My wife,** *wewawlee.* **Will you be my wife?,** *scothakeweitamee.*

Will, I will, *papiache, pawpiachee.*

Wind, *secacoonee.*

Winter, *pepokee.*

Wolf, a, *wyeewaw.*

Woman, *queakee.* **Woman, a,** *quiawaw.* **A young woman,** *meeaw-neequaw.* **An old woman,** *meakeybue-thetha.* **Pretty woman,** *olethey quiawa.*

Wood for fire, *teikou.*

Wyandot, a, *nottoweitha.*

Year, a, *kicotto.*

Yellow, *outhaw-wee.* **Gold or yellow money,** *outhaw-wee monie.*

Yes, *a-a, enee.*

Yesterday, *oulacon.*

You, *kealaw.*

Numerical Table

1. Nicoutee.
2. Nisswee.
3. Theywe.
4. Neawee.
5. Nealanawey.
6. Necotothwey.
7. Nesothwey.
8. Thyawsicthewy.
9. Chagathwey.
10. Metaghthwey.

11. Metaghtheney keteneycoutey.
12. Metaghtheney keteneyswee.
13. Metaghtheney ketenthwea.
14. Metaghtheney keteneawey.
15. Metaghtheney keteneallauwey.
16. Metaghtheney ketenecoutothwey.
17. Metaghtheney ketenesoythwey.
18. Metaghtheney ketensoyuricothwey.
19. Metaghtheney ketenchawgaththwea.

20. Necoutothwey, or Neaswawpeatatache.
30. Thyawpeytockkee.
40. Newawpetockkee.
50. Nea allanwawpetockkee.
60. Neekatyawsee.
70. Neesyawsee.
80. Thyawsee.
90. Chawa-ka.
100. Tepea-away.

200. Neasinee tepea-away.
300. Thenee tepea-away.
400. Neawee tepea-away.
500. Neallany tepea-away.
600. Necoutoyththeni tepea-away.
700. Nessoyththeni tepea-away.
800. Chawaka tepea-away.

1000. Metagththeney tepea-away.

49

CLASSIFICATION OF THE ALGONQUIAN LANGUAGES

ALGONQUIAN
   Blackfoot
   CREE-MONTAGNAIS
      CREE
      MONTAGNAIS-NASKAPI
   ARAPAHOAN
      ARAPAHO-GROS VENTRE
      Nawathinehena
   Cheyenne
   Menominee
   OJIBWAYAN
      NORTHERN OJIBWA
         Severn Ojibwa
         Northern Algonquin
      SOUTHERN OJIBWA
         Saulteaux
         Central Southern Ojibwa
         Old Algonquin
         Ottawa
      Potawatomi
   SAUK-FOX-KICKAPOO
      Sauk-Fox
      Kickapoo
   Shawnee
   Miami-Illinois
   EASTERN ALGONQUIAN, etc.

Source: Goddard 1996

Also available in the American Language Reprint Series

Volume 1. A Vocabulary of the Nanticoke Dialect
Volume 2. A Vocabulary of Susquehannock
Volume 3. A Vocabulary of the Unami Jargon
Volume 4. A Vocabulary of Powhatan
Volume 5. An Ancient New Jersey Indian Jargon
Volume 6. A Vocabulary of Tuscarora
Volume 7. A Vocabulary of Woccon
Volume 8. A Dictionary of Powhatan
Volume 9. A Vocabulary of Mohegan-Pequot
Volume 10. A Vocabulary of New Jersey Delaware
Volume 11. A Vocabulary of Stadaconan
Volume 12. Denny's Vocabulary of Delaware
Volume 13. A Vocabulary of Roanoke
Volume 14. Denny's Vocabulary of Shawnee
Volume 15. Cummings' Vocabulary of Delaware
Volume 16. Early Vocabularies of Mohawk
Volume 17. Schoolcraft's Vocabulary of Oneida
Volume 18. Elliot's Vocabulary of Cayuga
Volume 19. Schoolcraft's Vocabulary of Onondaga
Volume 20. Elliot's Vocabulary of Mohawk
Volume 21. Cummings' Vocabulary of Shawnee
Volume 22. A Vocabulary of Seneca
Volume 23. The Tutelo Language
Volume 24. Handy's Vocabulary of Miami
Volume 25. Observations on the Mahican Language
Volume 26. Minor Vocabularies of Tutelo and Saponi
Volume 27. Wood's Vocabulary of Massachusett
Volume 28. Chew's Vocabulary of Tuscarora
Volume 29. Early Fragments of Minsi Delaware
Volume 30. A Vocabulary of Wyandot
Volume 31. Heckewelder's Vocabulary of Nanticoke
Volume 32. Minor Vocabularies of Huron
Volume 33. Castiglioni's Vocabulary of Cherokee
Volume 34. Elements of a Miami-Illinois Grammar
Volume 35. Ridout's Vocabulary of Shawnee
Volume 36. A Vocabulary of Stockbridge Mahican
Volume 37. Minor Vocabularies of Nanticoke-Conoy
Volume 39. A Vocabulary of Etchemin
Volume 40. A Vocabulary of the Souriquois Jargon

For more information on the series, see our website at:
www.evolpub.com/ALR/ALRbooks.html

www.ingramcontent.com/pod-product-compliance
Lightning Source LLC
Chambersburg PA
CBHW022031090426
42739CB00006BA/381